Loving Babies

Kathryn Hollins, Anna Cox, Michelle McDermott, Ali F. Jabeen & Elfrida Society Parents Project

illustrated by Lisa Kopper

series editor Sheila Hollins

Beyond Words

Leatherhead

1

2

3

4

5

6

7

8

9

10

11

12

13

14

15

16

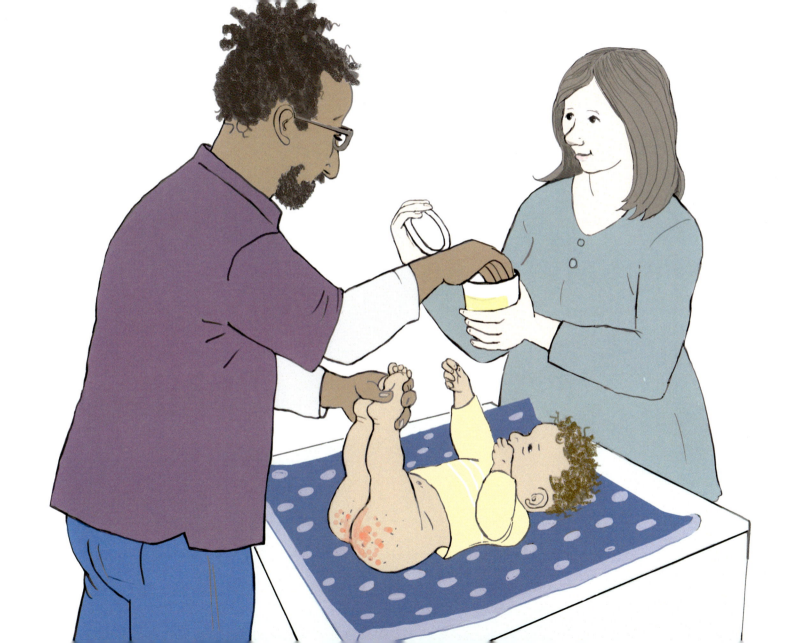

17

18

19

20

21

22

23

24

25

26

27

28

29

30

31

32

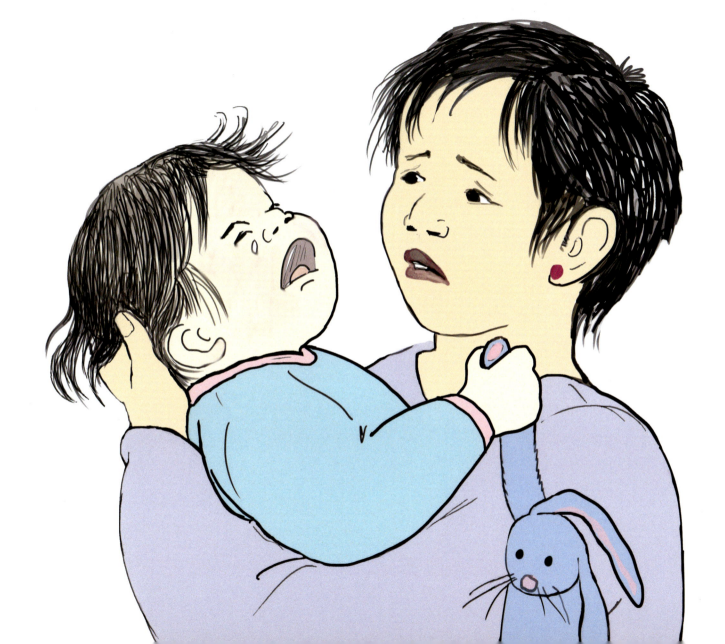

33

34

35

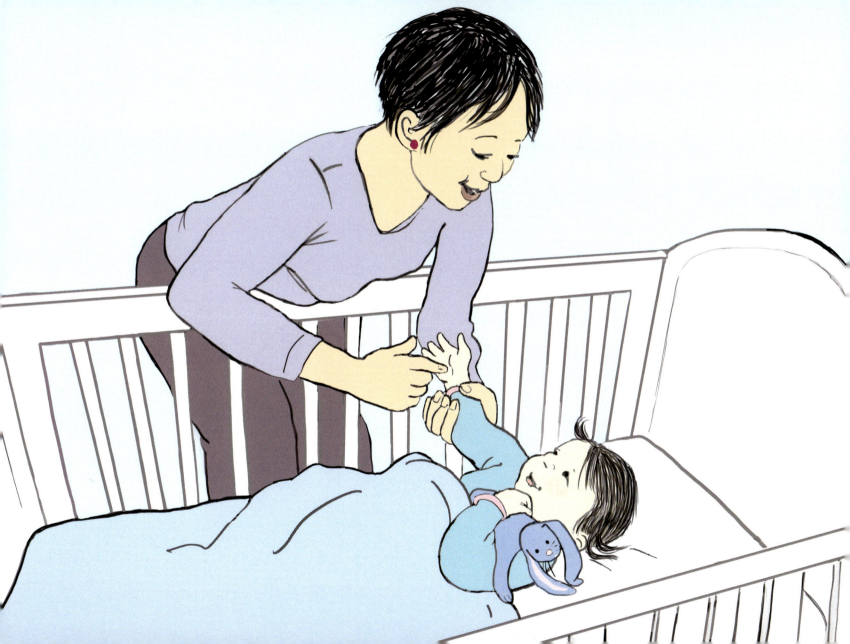

36

37

38

39

40

41

Authors and Artist

Dr Kathryn Hollins helps families create trusted relationships so that babies, children and parents can develop lifelong health and happiness. Kathryn is a mother herself and works as a consultant parent, child and family psychiatrist and psychotherapist in Surrey (Best Start Programme: pregnancy to age five). She also meets families in her own independent clinic and offers online parenthood resources: **www.drkathrynhollins.com**

Dr Anna Cox is a chartered psychologist and Senior Lecturer in the School of Health Sciences at the University of Surrey. Anna leads the Together Project that focuses on co-producing resources to improve care for parents with learning disabilities www.surrey.ac.uk/togetherproject

Michelle McDermott is an expert by experience who works at Paradigm co-delivering training to support parents with learning difficulties and disabilities www.paradigm-uk.org. She is a Co-Chairperson at Thera Trust www.thera.co.uk. As Michelle is a person with lived experience and a learning disability on Thera Trust's Board, she enjoys sharing her experiences, skills and knowledge. Michelle facilitates a Beyond Words book club.

Ali F Jabeen has over 20 years experience working with individuals with learning difficulties and disabilities (LDD), both as a professional and expert by experience. She is an accredited parenting practitioner and specialist advocate. Ali was group facilitator for a peer support group within The Elfrida Society Parents Project (ESPP), which has been supporting LDD parents for an impressive 35 years in London **www.elfrida.com**

Lisa Kopper has had a long career in children's illustration, publishing and media. This is the 10th story in the Books Beyond Words series that Lisa has illustrated. She currently lives and works in Bristol, UK.

Series Editor

Sheila Hollins is the Founder, Lead Editor and Executive Chair of Beyond Words, and a Family Carer. She is Emeritus Professor of Psychiatry of Disability at St George's, University of London, and is a Member of the House of Lords. She is a past President of the Royal College of Psychiatrists, the British Medical Association and the Royal College of Occupational Therapists.

Acknowledgments

We are grateful for the generous support and advice of all our advisors. Special thanks to the people who read drafts of the picture story, including: the parent members of The Elfrida Society Parents Project; Beyond Words book club members in Kent and South London (as part of Generate); Alexis Quinn; Dorabella Hollins; students from Henshaws Specialist College; a group from Macintyre i4t; children from Laithwaites and Kexborough Primary Schools in Barnsley; a student from Paternoster Special School in Cirencester; a student from Forest Oak Special School; a member of the Plymouth Parent Advisory Project. Grateful thanks to Hannah Pimble, and to Laura Cook, our Book Coordinator.

Finally, we are grateful to Porticus for their financial support and enthusiasm for both this book and the companion book, called *Having a Baby*.

First published in the UK 2023 by Books Beyond Words.

Text & illustrations © Books Beyond Words, 2023.

No part of this book may be reproduced in any form, or by any means, without the prior permission in writing from the publisher.

ISBN 978-1-78458-166-4

British Library Cataloguing-in-Publication Data

A catalogue record for this book is available from the British Library.

Printed by Royal British Legion Industries, Leatherhead.

Books Beyond Words is a Charitable Incorporated Organisation (no. 1183942).

Further information about the Books Beyond Words series can be obtained from Beyond Words' website: www.booksbeyondwords.co.uk.

Information and Resources

We would love to share more about ways of reading and using this book. We also have information and links to some excellent resources for parents, babies, families and practitioners.

Please visit **https://booksbeyondwords.co.uk/s/BBW-Loving-Babies-Resources** or use the QR code on this page.